C000096288

# SCHOOL'S OUT

# SCHOOL'S OUT

*Truants, troublemakers and teachers' pets*

JAMES THELLUSSON

SANDSTONE PRESS

First published in Great Britain in 2022 by
Sandstone Press Ltd
PO Box 41
Muir of Ord
IV6 7YX
Scotland

www.sandstonepress.com

ISBN: 978-1-913207-65-6
ISBNe: 978-1-913207-66-3

Sandstone Press is committed to a sustainable future.
This book is made from Forest Stewardship Council ® certified
paper.

Cover design by Jason Anscomb
Typeset by Iolaire Typesetting, Newtonmore
Printed and bound in Great Britain
by TJ Books Limited, Padstow, Cornwall

*To Jenny, Abi, Ben and 'Hud'*
*for encouraging me to try harder*

# CONTENTS

# FOREWORD

*'There has been a cheerful absence of effort in
all his work.'*

ANON

Stephen Fry says that his school reports were
'florid' in their criticisms of his bad behaviour.
P.G. Wodehouse was chastised for writing 'silly'
rhymes in his classmates' books. Joanna Lumley
remembers school for 'horrible maths'.

School reports are a snapshot of our school days
and a trigger for youthful memories, good and
bad. They are a window into who we are, or were,
and a source of colourful biographical detail.
Vignettes in vinegar, you might say. And it's this
aspect of the school report that makes them fasci-
nating. Kind they often are not, but their cruelty
is part of what makes them appealing.

Sadly, too many school reports have been lost
to history, burnt in bonfires or buried in boxes
hidden in attics around the country. *School's Out*
is an attempt to stem this loss of biographical

biodiversity by collecting together some of the best and worst school reports of Britain's Royal Family, politicians, comedians and other A-listers since the 18th century.

*School's Out* also includes waspish reports from ordinary folk, who willingly submitted their own school reports in response to my research requests. This is the first book to combine the reports of the rich and famous with those of more ordinary mortals. It proves Will Rogers, the actor, was right to say, 'everybody is ignorant, only on different subjects.' To readers of *The Oldie*, its editor Harry Mount, and everyone else who sent me their reports, I send my sincere gratitude.

A final note. Education has evolved since *Tom Brown's School Days*, when it was okay to roast your classmates in front of a fire and caning was rife across all sectors of the education system. This is not a history book but the material reflects the values and cultures of the institutions from which it comes. It shows some were encouraged, included and inspired by their schools and teachers. Others faced glass ceilings and prejudice. This anthology reflects both experiences.

# THE CAUSTIC QUILL AWARDS

*In days gone by, writers talked of dipping their quills in bile before writing satirical or caustic pieces. The Caustic Quill Awards is my selection of the best of the worst school reports: each drips with vinegar and few could or would be written now.*

**Charlotte Brontë**: 'Writes indifferently.'

**Anon**: 'This term in Religious Studies we have studied different religions and gods. [*They*] wrote an engaging and enthusiastic piece about Wayne Rooney.'

**Sir Billy Connolly**, comedian: 'I taught your father, and he was an idiot, too.'

**Anon**: 'She will start the next term unencumbered by any prior knowledge.'

**R. Davis**: 'If this boy spent half as much time doing work instead of finding ways of avoiding the task, he could do well.'

**Prince Albert Victor**: 'Apathetic with an abnormally dormant mind.'

**C. Durnford**, as a young sub-lieutenant in the Royal Navy: 'A tired-looking officer who gives the impression that the working day is interrupting his sex life.'

**Giles Fraser**, priest: 'Like a monkey, [Giles] is intent on displaying himself from his least attractive angle.'

**Anon**: 'The only thing original about this essay is the spelling.'

**Richard Heller**, journalist: 'It's not just the cream that floats to the top. It's the scum too.'

**Anon**: 'He has tended to adopt a silly approach to his achievements even to the extent of making a mock show of delight in low marks.'

**Jon Snow**, broadcaster: 'Has set himself low standards, which he fails to meet.'

**K. Nottage**: 'He is his own worst enemy, though he continues to believe that I am.'

**Anon**: 'He can learn nothing till he has learnt to attend.'

**F. Nolan**: 'I have failed to change his attitude from mind-numbingly neutral, despite my attempts at anger, humour, threats, irony, heavy sarcasm etc.'

**J. Aldridge**: 'I would be grateful if Julia would sometimes allow me to take the class.'

# THE GREAT BRITISH
# SCHOOL REPORT

The earliest school reports were literally letters written by the headmaster or a tutor to the parents of the children in their care. This report written by the headmaster of Winchester in 1728 typifies the elegant style of the school report at the time:

*'The custom of the place which requires us every year to give the Parents of Children instructed with us an account of their behaviour and progress in learning, furnishes me with an opportunity of paying my respects to yourself, which I am assured will be very acceptable to you, that I am perfectly pleased with the proceedings of your three boys. They attend their business very carefully, are very obedient to all the Rules of the place, and each of them has made as good a Progress in their learning as can be expected from the short time, they have been with us, and the disadvantages of their former methods put them under.'*

As the 19<sup>th</sup> century progressed, schools introduced a more systematic and structured report card and the letter style report disappeared, though at Eton reports are still nicknamed 'Letters' today. Instead, school reports included exam results by subject along with a few words of encouragement or criticism from the teachers.

How many of these letter style reports made it home we will never know. But, at The King's School, Canterbury, slackers could not hide their poor results because the school published a league table of exam results in the local paper.

Over time, parents demanded greater accountability from schools. Teachers responded by producing reports on each academic subject as well as extra-curricular subjects like games, debating, arts and drama. This interest in the wider development of pupils was the result of Victorian educationalists, like Matthew Arnold, asking new questions about the purpose of education and an interest in developing pupils with the so-called 'character' to run the Country and defend the Empire.

By the start of the 20<sup>th</sup> century, school reports included judgements about the character of pupils, their ethics and their chances of succeeding at 'life'. Teachers believed they were 'in loco parentis' and felt empowered to express their anger, affection and admiration for individuals, in ways which would now seem unprofessional and foolish. Through the century, education philosophy shifted and a new view of the purpose of school reports appeared. By the 1990s, character judgements had been expelled and a more factual approach to report writing arrived.

Some say this modern regime is too 'PC' and gives children and parents a false picture of their child's progress (or lack of it). Others say it is not the job of a teacher to make subjective judgements about children or undermine their aspirations. As several of the entries in this book reveal, a lack of success at school does not predict lack of success in life.

### NOT THE END OF THE WORLD

In 2013, comedian Sarah Millican, who went to Mortimer comprehensive, tweeted to students about to get their A level results: 'good luck but it isn't the end of the world if you don't get what you want. I got a D and E.' Other celebs who have taken to Twitter to reassure young people that bad exam results don't define them include comedian Russell Brand, who described the system as 'rhubarb', Deborah Meaden of *Dragon's Den*, and Goggleboxer Scarlett Moffatt, who confessed she had to take Maths three times before getting into university.

# TROUBLEMAKERS

*'I have admitted lately a big boy who seems to behave like an idiot, plays truant, makes ugly faces and hinders work here: I am studying the lad carefully, to see if anything can be done for him.'*

HEADMASTER OF KING WILLIAM STREET, 1899

## Climbing a tree naked

HUMPHRY BERKELEY (1926–1994)
*Malvern College & University of Cambridge*

Berkeley, who went on to become Conservative MP for Lancaster, invented a boarding school called Selhurst. Pretending to be its fictional headmaster, Berkeley wrote letters to the head-masters of famous public schools with absurd requests hoping to hoax them. When his decep-tion unravelled, Berkeley was expelled from Cambridge. The letters were later published as *The Life and Death of Rochester Sneath*.

# Disgraceful and lazy

SIR PETER BOTTOMLEY MP (b.1944)
*Westminster School & University of Cambridge*

At junior high school in Washington D.C., Bottomley received a 'less than flattering school report'. His mother consoled him that a report which said 'would do better if he tried harder' was preferable to one which said 'trying as hard as possible, still useless'. Bottomley later studied Economics at Trinity College. 'For years afterwards I would write to my college tutor and Dean, the divine Rev Harry Williams, who lived with the monks at Mirfield, apologising for being his most disgraceful and lazy undergraduate.'

# Threw an inkwell

ANEURIN BEVAN (1897–1960)
*Sirhowy Elementary & Central Labour College, London*

Bevan left school aged 13, though he later studied Marxism at the Plebs League, an organisation which promoted an understanding of Marxist thinking. According to Lord Kinnock, Bevan's stammer came about because of bullying from his school headmaster, who once hit him on the chin. Bevan responded by stamping on the teacher's corns. On another occasion, Bevan threw an inkwell at the headmaster for mocking a poor student because his brother was absent from school. The reason for his absence? The family only had one pair of shoes which the boys had to share, meaning only one of them could come to school on any single day. Bevan's indignation is perhaps an early sign of his willingness to fight against the social order and its uncaring attitude.

## Prison or a millionaire

SIR RICHARD BRANSON (b.1950)
*Stowe School*

Branson's headmaster's parting words were, 'Congratulations, Branson. I predict that you will either go to prison or become a millionaire.'

**D. Crook**: 'Thoroughly unsatisfactory. She is indolent, late and badly behaved.' A year later things had not improved much: 'Diana's behaviour has been most disappointing this term. With more sincere ambition and higher moral standards she should do well.'

## Like a monkey at the zoo

GILES FRASER (b.1964)
*Uppingham School &*
*Newcastle and Lancaster Universities*

Priest and broadcaster Fraser's tutor wrote, 'Like a monkey at the zoo, Giles is intent on displaying himself from his least flattering angle. His chief social assets are spitting and swearing. His house master is discovering that it is possible to avoid him but there are others, however, who are less fortunate.'

## The King of Pranksters?

HORACE DE VERE COLE (1881–1936)
*Eton College & University of Cambridge*

De Vere Cole was so notorious for his pranks that a silent movie was made about him called *Stolen Orders* (1918). His most infamous con involved impersonating an Abyssinian King and tricking Admiral May into giving him an 'access all areas' tour of HMS *Dreadnought*, including a slap-up Royal Navy tea. The prank was exposed by the *Daily Express*, much to the shame of the Admiral and the Royal Navy, whose gullibility and poor security protocols were exposed. At Cambridge,

De Vere Cole was friendly with Captain Lawrence Oates, who died attempting to reach the North Pole with Scott of the Antarctic. Both climbed the college roofs of Cambridge at night with George Winthrop Young, another infamous prankster and author of *The Roof-Climber's Guide to Trinity.*

**M. Hudson**: 'He is not content to remain unheard in the form room: his views are soon known; he also has an annoying habit of being sycophantic when he is actually behaving ... the locust years have taken their toll.'

## I was too advanced for school

ARTHUR HARDING (1886–1981)
*Schools Unknown*

Harding was born in 1886 into a poor, working class family who lived in one of the most infamous slums in Victorian London – 'The Nichol' – in Bethnal Green. He says he 'studied' hard to be a criminal and graduated quickly from pickpocketing to leading a notorious gang. He might have taken a different route though. In his autobiography, he says he left school, aged 11, 'after a series of examinations by a Board School inspector, [found] I was far too advanced for the L.C.C. [London County Council] school ... the authorities did not trouble whether I went to school or not, so I was allowed the freedom of the streets.'

## It was war every day

TOM ILUBE CBE (b.1963)
*Edo College, Benin & University of Benin*

Technology entrepreneur Ilube says, 'My maths teacher was the best teacher of my life.' He did not get on as well with his science teacher, who reported, 'Tom is a very capable lad, but he is a great source of distraction to others and resents rebuke very strongly and spends a lot of lesson time sulking. A pity.' Ilube says, 'I was actually always fascinated by science so much that I went on to get a degree in Applied Physics. But I really didn't get on with that science master. It was war every day. To be honest, most of the work was trivially easy, so I felt my main duty at school was to make the lives of anyone who sat near me as entertaining as possible. I hope life worked out for the poor souls who sat next to me (sorry guys, wherever you are!).'

## Keep away from him

JOHN LENNON (1940–1980)
*Quarry Bank High School & Liverpool College of Art*

Lennon's teachers said he had 'too many wrong ambitions and his energy is often misplaced'. He said: 'I was the one who all the other boys' parents – including Paul's [McCartney] – would say, "Keep away from him" ... The parents instinctively recognised I was a troublemaker, meaning I did not conform, and I would influence their children, which I did.' Lennon failed his O levels and dropped out of Liverpool College of Art.

## First political protest

DAVID LLOYD GEORGE,
1ST EARL LLOYD-GEORGE (1863–1945)
*Llanystumdwy National School*

Lloyd George was a passionate non-conformist from his school days. He organised his first political protest at his Anglican foundation school stirring up the other boys to refuse to say the catechism in front of visiting dignitaries. Lloyd George spoke Welsh as his mother tongue and is the only British Prime Minister to date not to speak English as his first language.

## Talking in tongues

BERNARD MANNING (1930–2007)
*Mount Carmel School, Manchester*

The comedian used to claim that he talked so much in class that his teachers nicknamed him 'Bernard Long-tongue'.

## Naughty not wicked

MIRIAM MARGOLYES OBE (b.1941)
*Oxford High School & University of Cambridge*

At school, Margolyes loved French. Her French teacher described her as 'naughty' but not 'wicked'. She read English at Newnham College and represented it on *University Challenge*. Rumour says she was the first person to say 'fuck' on the show.

## You simply do not exist

SIR JONATHAN MILLER CBE (1934–2019)
*St Paul's & University of Cambridge*

Asked to submit a memory to the school magazine, Miller wrote of a subversive magazine he started with peers in the Literary Society called the *Prickly Pear.* 'As far as I can remember, it was meant to express a direly nihilistic view of life in general ... but I can't recall anything which justified the abrupt repression which was almost immediately called down upon it. Almost before it could be distributed, two of us were summoned to the high master's office where we were told quite firmly that such a thing was simply not on and that for reasons which he was not prepared to divulge, the magazine was to be destroyed. As for the literary society itself he said, "You simply do not exist". As I write these lines, the memory of that occasion revives a resentment which has remained unextinguished for more than 30 years.'

## Explosive Stuff

DR STANLEY ORMAN (b.1935)
*Hackney Downs Boys School & University of London*

Orman almost had his university admission ruined by his headmaster. 'In my final year, using the freedom of the chemistry laboratory I made a sensitive explosive that was harmless when wet. Another pupil sprinkled some on the head-master's private staircase, thus convincing the pompous ass of an attempt on his life. I admitted making the material, denied being responsible for the placement, and refused to identify the perpetrator. The Head threatened to withdraw testimonials he had sent to university for me. However, he did not follow through.' Much later, Orman became an Undersecretary of State and developed Britain's nuclear deterrent.

**F. Nolan**: 'Work in class is slow at the best of times and, if sitting next to another pupil, is stationary. Geography is an unwelcome intrusion into [his] life. Especially when work is expected from him. I have failed to change his attitude from mind-numbingly neutral.'

## Dishonourable discharge

SIMON SPRACKLING (b.1960)
*Colston's School & Universities of Bristol and Edinburgh*

Simon Sprackling was a menace at school. Prior to being expelled, he was kicked out of the Combined Cadet Forces (CCF). He confesses: 'While conducting drill training, I deliberately marched two groups of junior cadets into one another, resulting in a huge fight. The furious

Captain of the CCF wrote to my father, a colonel in the British Army at the time, explaining that I was going to receive a Dishonourable Discharge. My Dad wrote back saying: "As a military man yourself, you will know there are only three reasons for a Dishonourable Discharge: rape, buggery and cowardice under fire. Which of these has he committed? Or is it all three?"' The discharge was overturned. Sprackling did not follow his father into the army.

## Not the most tractable boy

THOMAS PAINE (1737–1809)
*Thetford Grammar School*

The author of the *Rights of Man* was an individualist at school who was described as far from 'tractable and docile' though also 'an apt and ready scholar'.

## The education of a dog

JONATHAN SWIFT (1667–1745)
*Kilkenny Grammar School & Trinity College, Dublin*

Swift was home schooled by his uncle Godwin. Asked by the Archdeacon of Dublin how he rated the education his uncle had paid for, Swift peevishly replied, 'He gave me the education of a dog.' The archdeacon replied, 'Then you have not the gratitude of a dog.' At Trinity, Swift was suspended for 'exciting disturbances within the college and insulting the junior dean'.

## An awful waste of time

LORD TAVERNE (b.1928)
*Charterhouse & University of Oxford*

Lord Taverne was an independent thinker even at school. 'We had to take part in a competition between house platoons of the school "Corps" and attack an enemy defending a hilltop. Our house, "Pageites", was unenthusiastic about military training. I was [in charge] as "acting lance corporal" and suggested we should not waste lovely summer afternoons on this ridiculous exercise and, instead, find a secluded spot to laze in, hidden from the officious master in charge Major Morris. On competition day, I asked one platoon member [to find] the enemy hilltop. When it was our turn to attack, the supervising Sandhurst cadet told us to march off. I told Pageites to follow me at a run in a different direction, from which the enemy would not expect [us]. The Sandhurst cadet shouted "Stop! They don't know you are attacking." But we surged on and overwhelmed the enemy without a hostile shot fired. An operation scheduled to take 30 minutes was over in ten. The Sandhurst cadet was so impressed he recommended we win the cup, despite breaking all the rules! Major Morris exploded. He could not believe it. I was promoted and still have a pewter mug inscribed: Arthur Webster Cup, Winner Sergeant (!) Taverne.'

## Driven to rebellion

ANTHONY TROLLOPE (1815–1882)
*Harrow School*

Trollope won a scholarship to Harrow, a place he detested. 'As I look back it seems to me that all hands were turned against me, those of masters as well as boys. I was allowed to join in no plays. Nor did I learn anything, for I was taught nothing … I was never a coward and cared for a thrashing as little as any boy, but one cannot make a stand against the acerbities of three hundred tyrants without a moral courage of which at that time I possessed none. I know that I skulked and was odious to the eyes of those I admired and envied. At last, I was driven to rebellion, and there came a great fight, at the end of which my opponent had to be taken home for a while.'

---

**GREAT SCHOOL RIOTS**

**1710** Winchester: Scholars revolt at cuts to their beer rations in a two-week stand-off.

**1768** Eton: boys riot over restrictions to Prefects' rights.

**1771** Harrow: boys attack a visiting governor and the school closes for nine days.

**1797** Rugby: School rebellion ends after local army militia is called to the school.

**1818** Winchester: The warden is held hostage overnight by boys armed with axes.

**1851** Marlborough: a rebellion starts on Guy Fawkes Night with an explosion.

**1911** Pencil Strike: Pupils at 62 state schools demand shorter hours, attendance payments and free pencils.

**1969** LSE students occupy building in protest against the appointment of a new Governor with connections to apartheid Rhodesia (now Zimbabwe).

**2021** Pimlico Academy: Students protest at a new 'racist' school dress code which allegedly bans the afro.

---

## Played his nose

JOHNNY VEGAS (b.1970)
*St Joseph's College & Middlesex University*

Vegas went to a Catholic seminary boarding school. At school, he used to use his nose as a musical instrument to entertain his classmates and could perform Hawaiian style tunes on it. Vegas graduated from Middlesex University with a third-class degree in Ceramics and Pottery which he says usefully qualified him to mend tea pots.

## Never live like a slave

SIR WILLIAM WALLACE (1270–1305)
*High School, Dundee*

Wallace was a Scottish knight who fought the English, famously defeating them at Stirling Bridge in 1297. It is believed Wallace went to the High School, Dundee and learnt Latin at school including the lines *'Dico tibi verum, Libertas optima rerum, Nunquam servili, sub nexu vivito, fili'*: 'I tell you the truth when I say freedom is the best of all things. Sons, never live life like a slave.'

# Too much time in a cake shop

DAME JULIE WALTERS DBE (b.1950)
*Holly Lodge Grammar School &*
*Manchester School of Theatre*

Walters was asked to leave her grammar school 'mainly because I was never there'. When not at school she spent her time in a local cake shop with her best friend discussing life. After training to be a nurse, Walters went to drama school and is now one of the nation's favourite actresses.

# SCHOOLED TO RULE

*Of the 55 British Prime Ministers, 20 have been to Eton, seven to Harrow and six to Westminster. Only 10 have been educated at non-fee-paying schools.*

## The smiles of insolent scholars

NAPOLEON BONAPARTE (1769–1821)
*Military school in Brienne & Ecole Militaire, Paris*

Napoleon was teased by his aristocratic classmates at the military school in Paris for his dialect. His mother tongue was Corsican, so he spoke French with an unfashionable accent. Bonaparte came 42nd out of the 58 in his class at military school. The school reinforced the chip on his shoulder about his status in French society. He complained to his father: 'I am tired ... of seeing the smiles of insolent scholars who are only superior to me by reason of their fortune.' Refused by the Navy because of his poor exam ranking, Napoleon went into the Royal Artillery, aged 16, and went on to rewrite the map of Europe. Ironically, geography was his favourite subject at school.

**T. Beard**: 'A passing interest in French is less important than an interest in passing French.'

## Feeble and abnormal

EDWARD VII (1841–1910)
*Home schooled & Various universities*

Queen Victoria had Edward evaluated by a phrenologist, whose report stated Edward's skull was 'feeble and abnormal'. Queen Victoria was equally uncomplimentary, describing Edward's mind as 'empty'. Edward spent time at university in Edinburgh, Oxford and Cambridge but never graduated.

## Demanded sausages for 40

SIR WINSTON CHURCHILL (1874–1965)
*Harrow School & Royal Military Academy, Sandhurst*

Churchill's fiery temper is noted in a letter to school newspaper *The Harrovian* in 1929: '. . . an acquaintance of mine was acting as assistant in a certain Harrow tuck shop. One afternoon . . . she had to deal with a big and tempestuous customer who demanded "sausages, mashed potatoes and tea for 40 in an hour's time" [then] incontinently evaporated. The young assistant . . . sought advice from an acquaintance. "Oh, that was only Winston Churchill," she was told. "He only wants to give tea to his house. You get the stuff in as quick as you can."' Churchill, who won the Nobel Prize in Literature in 1953, was poor at maths and only managed to pass the exams to Sandhurst on his third attempt.

## Speaks French like English

QUEEN ELIZABETH I (1553–1603)
*Home schooled*

Elizabeth I was educated by Roger Ascham, the greatest educationalist of his time, who wrote that Elizabeth knew much of Cicero and Livy and that 'French and Italian she speaks like English, Latin with fluency [...] and Greek passably.' The 'Virgin Queen' also studied grammar, theology, history, rhetoric, logic, philosophy, maths, logic, literature and geometry.

# Art forgery?

PRINCE HARRY, DUKE OF SUSSEX (b.1984)
*Eton College & Royal Military School, Sandhurst*

Prince Harry was cited in an exam scandal when Sarah Forsyth, his art teacher at Eton, claimed she wrote the text to accompany the paintings the Prince had submitted for his A level art project. She made the claim in an unfair dismissal case. The employment tribunal found no evidence of cheating but accepted the Prince had received help in preparing his A level project. An examination board investigation cleared him of cheating.


# The wisest fool in Christendom?

JAMES VI & I (1566–1625)
*Home schooled*

James I acquired the nickname 'the wisest fool in Christendom' for failing to use his undoubted intellectual talents to manage his kingdom better. He certainly oversaw a 'Golden Age' in English Literature with poets and playwrights such as Shakespeare prospering in his reign. James wrote several books, including a compendium on witchcraft lore called *Daemonologie*. He was also famously responsible for supporting the translation of the Bible known as the King James Bible, which many consider the most poetic of its translations. His most controversial pamphlet was *The True Law of Free Monarchies,* in which he reasserted the notion of divine right, writing: 'The sovereign succeeds to his kingdom by right from God.'

## Only PM to play cricket

SIR ALEC DOUGLAS-HOME (1903–1995)
*Eton College & University of Oxford*

Douglas-Home is the only British Prime Minister to have played first-class cricket, though his batting and bowling were mediocre. Academically, Douglas-Home was equally modest, graduating with a third-class degree in Modern History. Cyril Connolly, an Eton contemporary, wrote he 'was a votary of the esoteric Eton religion, [a] sleepy boy who [was] showered with favours and crowned with all the laurels [and was] liked by the masters and admired by the boys without any apparent exertion on his part ... In the 18th century he would have become Prime Minister before he was thirty. As it was, he appeared honourably ineligible for the struggle of life.' Despite this, Douglas-Home was appointed Prime Minister by the Conservative party with minimal effort when then sitting PM Harold Macmillan stood down.

## Hardly knows the meaning of the words to read

PRINCE ALBERT VICTOR (1864–1892)
*Home schooled & University of Cambridge*

Prince Albert Victor's tutor – the Rev Dr John Dalton, who was tasked with teaching him reading, writing, maths, Latin and French – described the Prince as 'apathetic with an abnormally dormant condition of mind'. Despite this, he went to Trinity College, where another tutor wrote, 'I do not think he can possibly derive much benefit from attending lectures at Cambridge ... He hardly knows the meaning of the words *to read*.' Cambridge awarded the Royal Prince an honorary degree.

## Pride in the old alma mater

HERBERT HENRY ASQUITH, 1ST EARL OF
OXFORD AND ASQUITH (1852–1928)
*City of London School & University of Oxford*

Asquith flourished at City of London, an independent school, and won a scholarship to Balliol

College, Oxford where he gained a first-class degree in 1874. He admired his college and his fellow students at Balliol so highly (and perhaps himself by association) that on becoming PM, he proudly referred to the 'effortless superiority' of Balliol men in a speech.

---

**THE GENTLEMAN'S DEGREE**

A third-class degree is nicknamed the 'Gentleman's degree' because only people who can afford not to work after graduating can risk such a poor result. While most Prime Ministers attended university, there is a small group who did not: John Major; the Duke of Wellington; Benjamin Disraeli; David Lloyd George; Winston Churchill and James Callaghan. Gordon Brown is arguably the most academically successful PM as he is the only one to have completed a PhD.

---

## Orgies of bad spelling

LORD DON FOSTER (b.1947)
*Lancaster Royal Grammar School & Keele University*

In a speech to his old school, former Lib Dem MP Foster read out his worst school reports without realising the Conservative MP for Lancaster

(Dame Elaine Kellett-Bowman) was taking notes. 'Later ... I was arguing [in Parliament] that the recent [Conservative] Budget had done little to help education. I said teachers, governors and, most importantly, pupils will suffer. Dame Elaine spoke after me in the debate saying, "The remarks of the Hon. Member for Bath do not entirely surprise me ... His school report boded ill for the Liberal party." She then read out the bad bits of my reports which she had recorded from my school day speech in 1994: "Muddle-headed and impulsive ... Daft and illogical ... Does less than justice to work by indulging in irreverence and orgies of bad spelling." We cannot judge the quality of his spelling now, but we can judge the quality of his logic.' Her remarks certainly didn't enhance my status as [Liberal Democrat] spokesman on Education.'

## Aeschylus in a shell hole

HAROLD MACMILLAN, 1ST EARL OF
STOCKTON (1894–1986)
*Eton College & University of Oxford*

Macmillan could understand French, Latin and Greek before he was seven years old and won an exhibition to study Classics at Balliol College. While waiting wounded in a shell hole at the Somme, he passed the time calmly reading a copy of Aeschylus' *Prometheus Bound* in the Ancient Greek, a book he had adored since school and carried with him throughout the war.

**G. Morris**: 'Graham was a loyal member of the school orchestra, as librarian.'

## Disgracefully cavalier

BORIS JOHNSON (b.1964)
*Eton College & University of Oxford*

Johnson was a King's Scholar at Eton and won a scholarship to read Classics at Balliol College. At Eton, his House Master wrote: 'Boris really has adopted a disgracefully cavalier attitude to his classical studies ... Boris sometimes seems affronted when criticised for what amounts to a gross failure of responsibility (and surprised at the same time that he was not appointed Captain of the School). I think he honestly believes that it is churlish of us not to regard him as an exception, one who should be free of the network of obligation which binds everyone else.'

## The beauty of his own voice

BARON MICHAEL GRADE OF YARMOUTH
(b.1943)
*Northcliffe House Prep School*

His music teacher reported, 'Grade is a valued member of the chapel choir, but has a habit of drifting into a trance, perhaps at the beauty of his own performance.'

## They howled me down

JAMIE STONE MP (b.1954)
*Gordonstoun School & University of St Andrews*

Stone remembers his first school mock-election in 1970. 'My English Teacher, Jack "Tar" Paterson, chose me in the Tain Royal Academy school mock-election as the Tory candidate. I mobbed it up something shocking, right down to [wearing] a tailcoat and top hat with my school shirt collar turned up Victorian-style. The [boys] howled me down, the rotten lot, and who heckled me worst of all? The son of my teacher – these days better known as Professor Lindsay Paterson of Edinburgh University, now a friend. Of course, I romped home with, er ... Let me quote from a poem in the school magazine:

*And poor defeated "Stoney"*
*Cursed at all these unjust men*
*Who must have cheated this good chap*
*To give him eight and ten!'*

## Wisely I didn't keep my reports

BARON DAVID TRIESMAN (b.1943)
*Stationers' Company's School &*
*Universities of Essex and Cambridge*

Asked if he would submit any of his school reports to this anthology, Lord Triesman, a banker and former head of the Football Association, replied: 'I fear I can't help. I wisely didn't keep any of my school reports.'

## Unclassified in the treasury

ANDY REED OBE (b.1964)
*Longsdale Community College &*
*De Montfort University*

Reed won an OBE for services to sport. His school PE report said: 'Although not abounding in skill, Andy makes up for this with his speed and determination.' Reed struggled with maths at school. 'I got a U for O level Maths. I used to laugh at the memory of it when I moved into the [Labour] Treasury ministerial team. I always expected a snarky newspaper headline. But one never came.'

## The quality of our legislators

LORD CLIVE SOLEY (b.1939)
*Downshall Secondary School & Universities of Strathclyde and Southampton*

In 1953, Soley's class teacher remarked, 'Clive's limited abilities could produce far better results if he made the great effort needed. His effort at present can only be described as half-hearted.' Of this anthology, Lord Soley remarked: 'I hope the public don't get too depressed by the quality of their legislators.'

## Deserves to do well

BARONESS MARGARET THATCHER (1925–2013)
*Grantham Girls' Grammar School & University of Oxford*

Britain's first female Prime Minister won a scholarship to Grantham Girls' Grammar School and was the school's star scientist. Her final report prophetically concludes, 'Margaret is ambitious and deserves to do well.' Thatcher is the only British Prime Minister to have held a Science degree.

## She deserves extra privileges

DUCHESS OF WINDSOR (1896–1986)
*Oldfields School (Maryland, USA)*

A note to her parents suggests Wallis Simpson was clever. In a 1914 report home the school said: 'We will give Wallis the privilege of going into town on Wednesday afternoon on the 2.20 train to have her skirt fitted. She has been such a faithful student and her averages have been so good we feel that she deserves some extra privileges.'

# ARTISTS AND WRITERS

*'He has a natural feel for words, but he should not let this excuse him from the necessary disciplines of writing. In particular, he is averse from writing in sentences.'*

ANON

## No nonsense about sport

ERIC AMBLER OBE (1909–1998)
*Colfe Grammar School & The Engineering College*

Ambler, the father of the modern British spy novel, loved science at school. 'I liked the discipline of science. The only discipline I did like.' He admitted he could 'never turn my hand to trig. Algebra, yes, I adored algebra. It's solving things, like chemistry, it's finding out. But I hated trig.' There are rumours Ambler was expelled for reading obscene poems. If true, it did not undermine his regard for his old school. 'There was no nonsense about compulsory sport. You were left alone ... The teaching was extraordinarily good.'

# Shuffles across his stumps

SAMUEL BECKETT (1906–1989)
*Portora Royal School & Trinity College, Dublin*

Beckett excelled at sports. His cricket coach criticised him for stepping out of his crease to hit the ball, a habit frowned upon at the time, but other reports note his 'stylish shots'. He played cricket twice for Trinity against Northamptonshire, making him the only winner of a Nobel Prize to play first-class cricket. After graduating, Beckett taught at a Protestant school in Belfast. Told he was privileged to be teaching the cream of Ulster's youth, Beckett said his pupils were, indeed, 'rich and thick'.

# No pleasure in boyish sports

SAMUEL TAYLOR COLERIDGE (1772–1834)
*Christ's Hospital School & University of Cambridge*

Coleridge 'took no pleasure in boyish sports' preferring to read. In *Biographia Literaria* he wrote, 'I enjoyed the inestimable advantage of a very sensible, though at the same time, a very severe master ... I learnt from him, that Poetry, even that of the loftiest ... had a logic of its own [...] he showed no mercy to phrase, metaphor, or image, unsupported by a sound sense, or where the same sense might have been conveyed with equal force and dignity in plainer words.'

## Knows nothing of grammar

CHARLOTTE BRONTË (1816–1855)
*Clergy Daughters' School*

Brontë went to the Clergy Daughters' School. A school report says she 'writes indifferently' and knew 'nothing of grammar, geography, history or accomplishments'.

## Annoyances at night

LEWIS CARROLL (1832–1898)
*Rugby School & University of Oxford*

At junior school Carroll's headmaster wrote '... a very uncommon share of genius ... he is capable of acquirements and knowledge far beyond his years, while his reason is so clear and so jealous of error, that he will not rest satisfied without the most exact solution of whatever appears to him obscure.' At Rugby, his mathematics teacher wrote 'I have not had a more promising boy at his age'. Carroll hated Rugby. 'I cannot say ...

that any earthly considerations would induce me to go through my three years again ... I can honestly say that if I could have been ... secure from annoyance at night, the hardships of the daily life would have been comparative trifles to bear.'

---

### JANE EYRE'S PORRIDGE

Victorian headmasters often pocketed the fees paid to them to feed their pupils and served inedible food as this extract from *Jane Eyre* shows. 'On two long tables smoked basins of something hot, which ... sent forth an odour far from inviting. I saw a universal manifestation of discontent when the fumes of the repast met the nostrils of those destined to swallow it ... the tall girls of the first class, rose the whispered words – "Disgusting! The porridge is burnt again!" ... burnt porridge is almost as bad as rotten potatoes; famine itself soon sickens over it. The spoons were moved slowly: I saw each girl taste her food and try to swallow it; but in most cases the effort was soon relinquished. Breakfast was over, and none had breakfasted.'

## A dream schoolboy

BENEDICT CUMBERBATCH CBE (b.1976)
*Harrow School & University of Manchester*

Cumberbatch was an arts scholar at Harrow but claims that his academic studies went off the rails once he discovered girls and other distractions in his teens. He made his school acting debut, aged 12, as Titania, Queen of the Fairies in *A Midsummer Night's Dream*. Cumberbatch's drama teacher is quoted as saying he was the best schoolboy actor he ever worked with.

**H. Ely**: 'All [the] art forgeries that he attempted were very good. I would encourage him to be more independent next year and focus on his own work ...'

## Your father was an idiot too

SIR BILLY CONNOLLY CBE (b.1942)
*St Peter's Boys School & St Gerard Secondary School*

Connolly remembers sitting in a puddle in the school playground and hearing his classmates laugh. He claims it made him want to become a comic. His teachers were far from funny, though. One used to say, 'I taught your father, and he was an idiot too.'

## Catching fleas with quills

CHARLES DICKENS (1812–1870)
*Wellington House Academy*

Has any British writer put school closer to the heart of their life and work than Dickens? Describing London in the mid-1840s as a 'vast hopeless nursery of ignorance, misery and vice' Dickens railed against the 'frightful neglect by the State of those … whom it might, as easily and less expensively, instruct and save'. Dickens campaigned tirelessly to raise funds for charitable organisations providing free education to poor children in 19th-century Britain. A visit to one in East London in 1843 inspired *A Christmas Carol*. Wackford Squeers, the headmaster in *Nicholas Nickleby*, was based on a real man, William Shaw, who was convicted of gross negligence after allowing eight boarders at his Yorkshire school to go blind yet was allowed to continue to run a boarding school. Dickens read the court reports about Shaw and his school, Bowes Academy, while researching the novel and incorporated the experiences of Shaw's pupils, including this diary extract from one pupil: 'Every other morning we used to flea the beds. The usher used to cut the quills and give us them to catch the fleas; and if you did not fill the quill, you caught a good beating. The pot-skimmings were called broth, and we used to have it for tea on Sunday; one of the ushers offered a penny a piece for every maggot, and there was a pot-full gathered: he never gave it them.'

---

### RIOTS AT RUGBY

1797: the boys of Rugby School rioted after their headmaster Dr Henry Inglis, a disciplinarian nicknamed the 'Black Tiger' for his vicious moods, ordered the boys pay to repair the windows of a shop which the retailer claimed they had broken. Instead of paying, the boys took up arms and rioted, chasing the headmaster with pen knives and burning school property. The situation – reminiscent of the final scene in Lindsay Anderson's film *If...* – was so anarchic the local Justice of the Peace read the boys the Riot Act and soldiers, special constables and farmers armed with horsewhips came to the school to restore order. The boys were eventually overcome, the ringleaders expelled, and several boys flogged.

## His ad-libbing was inspired

LAURENCE FOX (b.1978)
*Harrow School & Royal Academy of Dramatic Art*

At school, Fox was highly regarded as an actor and orator. In a debate between Harrow and Queenswood, an independent girls' school, in which he opposed the motion 'Does a fish need a bicycle?' *The Harrovian* reported 'Laurence Fox was the first to speak for Harrow and a single, crumpled sheet of A4 were the only notes he needed. I think it would be fair to say, therefore... that much of his clever wordplay was extemporised. But his ad-libbing was inspired. Indeed it was like watching another Laurence – Laurence Olivier – at work. When he ended ... an awed silence filled the room. When he sat, the audience sat with him.' Harrow and Fox won the debate.

## He blazed into me

GERARD MANLEY HOPKINS (1844–1889)
*Highgate School & University of Oxford*

Hopkins won a wager with a fellow pupil that he could survive twenty-one days without a drink of any sort. Unfortunately, betting was banned at the school, so when John Dyne, the headmaster, heard of the bet he asked Hopkins to return the money he had won. When Hopkins protested, he was beaten. Hopkins felt Dyne was prejudiced against him on other occasions. '[Dyne] had repeatedly said he hoped I might not be at the top of the school after the [Oxford] exams...' and he ejected Hopkins from the private room he had been given to revise for the Oxford entry. Angered, 'Dyne and I had a terrific altercation. I was driven out of patience and cheeked him wildly and he blazed into me with his riding whip.' Despite the efforts of his headmaster to nobble him, Hopkins won an exhibition to Balliol College, Oxford, where he gained a first-class degree in Classics.

## The court jester

SIMON KELNER (b.1957)
*Bury Grammar School & University of Central Lancashire*

Former *Independent* editor Kelner's English teacher reported that 'his written work is sound ... but he is far too eager to assume the role of court jester.' His form master reported he was 'an ebullient and extremely lively member of class, he adds a sparkle to a lesson. At times, however, his attitude degenerates into frippery.

I hope he has approached the exams seriously because he has very considerable ability and will do well in his chosen career.'

## No sense of rhythm

JOHN PAUL JONES (b.1946)
*Christ's College, London*

Along with Led Zeppelin's drummer, bassist John Paul Jones was part of one of the best rhythm sections in rock history. Ironically, his school sports coach said he was hopeless at swimming because he had 'no sense of rhythm'.

**R. Williams**: 'At ten, I desperately wanted to join my school choir. I failed the first audition but was given a second chance. A teacher listened to my heartfelt rendition of 'All Things Bright and Beautiful' and then realising who I was said, "oh no, not you again".'

## Flung himself on the floor

SIR HAROLD PINTER CBE (1930–2008)
*Hackney Downs Boys School &*
*Royal Academy of Dramatic Art*

A review of his school performance as Romeo says Pinter 'flung himself on the floor of the Friar's cell with histrionic passion'. A review of another play says, 'Master Pinter made a more eloquent, more obviously nerve-racked Macbeth than one or two professional grown-ups I have seen in the last two years.' Pinter also loved sports. He adored cricket and was chair of the Gaieties, a wandering cricket club, but at school his 'one real strength was sprinting'. Pinter broke the school

220 yards record and played centre forward in the football team, confessing he was 'on occasion a bit of a cheat'.

## Himmler of the lower fifth

SIR TERENCE RATTIGAN CBE (1911–1977)
*Harrow School & University of Oxford*

One teacher prophetically wrote: 'French execrable; theatre sense first class!' *The Harrovian*, reports Mr Crocker-Harris in *The Browning Version* is based on a teacher whom Rattigan nicknamed the 'Himmler of the Fifth Form'.

## Moved to tears

DEV PATEL (b.1990)
*Whitmore High School*

Best known as an actor, Patel has a bronze medal in Taekwondo won at the Action International Martial Arts Association World Championships (2004) as well as A levels in PE, Biology, History and Drama. His drama teacher says that Patel's live performance for his A*-rated GCSE moved the visiting examiner so much that he cried.

# Mouse in the bedroom

JOANNA LUMLEY DBE (b.1946)
*St Mary's Convent*

In her autobiography, Lumley says she kept a pet mouse at boarding school nicknamed 'Reepicheep', after the King of the Talking Mice in C.S. Lewis's *Narnia* books. She hid the mouse in her clothes drawer.

---

**NICEST INITIATION CEREMONY**

Harrow had an initiation ceremony in which new boys were provided with a 'florilegium', which means in Latin a 'selection of flowers'. The florilegium was not a bouquet but a collection of writings by famous writers designed to broaden arrivals' academic interest.

---

# A great autodidact

ALAN SILLITOE (1928–2010)
*Radford Boulevard Senior Boys' School*

Sillitoe wrote *Saturday Night and Sunday Morning* and *The Loneliness of the Long Distance Runner*, which transformed British novel writing after the Second World War. He left school aged

14 after failing to pass the entrance examinations to his local grammar school. He did not let this end his passion for literature and he devoured books incessantly while working at the Raleigh bike factory in Nottingham. This habit continued through his life and his friend, the writer Margaret Drabble, said he was one of the most widely read writers she had ever met.

## A fair knack of writing

EDWARD THOMAS (1878–1917)
*St Paul's School & University of Oxford*

At St Paul's, an independent school, Thomas's early reports describe him as 'backward' in Latin and having 'very little' Greek. His English reports said: 'Good. Has a memory for facts and a fair knack of writing.' Later his form master reported: 'I should say quite the ablest boy in the form considering his age. He has no taste for languages, but his history is very good.' He added: 'I wish he were a more sociable person.' The teacher had clearly spotted something in Thomas, who later liked to spend time alone, walking in the English countryside. Thomas won a scholarship to study History at Lincoln College, Oxford. He died after being shot through the chest in the Battle of Arras in 1917, just as he was coming of age as a poet.

## My bubble car got stuck in a snowdrift

ROBERT SPRACKLING (b.1962)
*Colston's School*

Writer of *Mike Bassett: England Manager*, Sprackling was difficult at school. 'I got beaten regularly. Reasons included "crawling down the chapel aisle making funny noises", "improbable excuses for being late for maths", and my favourite "My bubble car got caught in a snowdrift".'

## Stick to acting

SANDI TOKSVIG OBE (b.1958)
*Tormead School & University of Cambridge*

Toksvig read Law, Archaeology and Anthropology at Girton College, Cambridge where she was a leading member of the famous Footlights Dramatic Club. She graduated with a first-class degree and won two major academic prizes. She remembers telling her anthropology professor that she wanted to stay at Cambridge to do a

PhD. Her professor told her to 'have a glass of sherry and stick to acting'.

## Every inch a fool

SIR NORMAN WISDOM OBE (1915–2010)
*Children's Home, Kent*

Wisdom, a superstar of British film in the 1950s, was only 5'1" tall. His Army report said, 'This boy is every inch the fool; luckily for him he's not very tall.'

# GLASS CEILINGS AND CRAP CAREERS ADVICE

*Many now-famous figures were discouraged from pursuing their dreams by their school reports. This selection is a tribute to those who beat the odds and showed the naysayers what they could do.*

## Girls weren't even asked

SUE BLACK OBE (b.1962)
*Chelmer Valley High School &*
*London South Bank University*

As a child, Black saved her pocket money to buy maths textbooks. When she developed an interest in computing, she hit a problem. 'I get asked if I studied computing at school. I always say I was at school so long ago there wasn't any computing at school. Or that's what I thought until I met Netflix founder Neil Hunt. He went to a secondary school near mine and came to *my* school *for computing lessons* because his school didn't do computing. I guess girls at my school *weren't even asked* if they were interested in computing. But boys from other schools were coming to my school to be given computing lessons! I left school at 16 [and] I got there eventually. But how different my life could have been with more confidence and opportunity.'

## Don't go into design

EDWARD BARBER (b.1969)
*Leeds Polytechnic & Royal College of Art*

Barber and his business partner Jay Osgerby designed the London 2012 Olympic torch. Luckily, he ignored the advice of his D&T teacher who told him: 'I would not recommend a career in design.'

## Do a secretarial course

BARONESS BOYCOTT (b.1951)
*Cheltenham Ladies' College & University of Kent*

After founding the feminist magazine *Spare Rib*, Lady Boycott became the first female editor of a national newspaper when she took the helm at

*The Independent* in 1996. Years before, she left school with E grades in two A levels and was told to do a secretarial course as retaking her A levels at the school would be a waste of her time and theirs.

**L. Ely**: 'Any chance of a new skirt? The current one is outrageous ... Remember longer skirts mean higher grades!'

## You should be a boxer

NIRA CHAMBERLAIN OBE (b.1969)
*Turves Greens Boys' School &*
*Coventry Polytechnic*

Chamberlain had a passion for maths as a schoolboy and dreamed of becoming a professional mathematician. 'I was about 15 years old. I went to see my careers teacher. I said I wanted to do something which involved mathematics or logic. He said, "With a physique like yours you should be a boxer." When I told my parents, they said, "You don't need anyone's permission to be a great mathematician." That was not the last time I experienced racial prejudice. But when I have, I remember my parents' words. Your career should be determined by your ideas, not your race.' Later, he became President of the Institute of Mathematics and its Applications.

## Music will never pay

DAVID BOWIE (1947–2016)
*Burnt Ash Junior School &*
*Bromley Technical High School*

At junior school, Bowie's voice was described as 'adequate'. A secondary school report described Bowie as a quiet student who needed to realise that a career in music would never pay.

## Computers are the thing!

LORD DANNATT CBE (b.1950)
*St Lawrence College &*
*Royal Military School, Sandhurst*

'My housemaster was a delightful Anglican priest who had served with distinction in the Royal Navy in WW2 and [won] a Distinguished Service Cross. We adored and respected him, but careers advice was not his strong point. He had heard computers were the future so suggested I consider becoming a computer programmer, although neither he nor I knew what this meant. Then, he suggested I do the Oxbridge exams [to] read Law and become a barrister. I wanted to join the Army, so we compromised – I did the Oxbridge exams and was called to Emmanuel College. But by design or circumstance I put my foot in my mouth at the interview and was politely told "Perhaps, Mr Dannatt, you are more suited to joining the Police Force than reading Law at this college!" So, the following September, I joined the Army. The rest is history!'

## Economics changed my life

BARONESS MOLLY MEACHER (b.1940)
*Berkhamsted School for Girls &*
*Universities of York and London*

'I was sent to school aged 10. At the time my educational level was five years behind my age group. I felt a complete dunce. By my O level year, I had caught up. I passed nine O levels. Nevertheless, the headmistress told my parents it would be a waste of the school's time *and* mine to remain at the school to take A levels.' After school, she decided to study Economics. 'My then husband, Michael Meacher (a Labour MP) turned up, not with flowers but a bunch of economics books. I thought, oh my goodness I really think I will try and go to University. It was a frightening thought. After all, I was a dunce! Nine months later I took my A levels.' Meacher was pregnant when she passed her A levels by correspondence course. She now has degrees from the University of York and the University of London.

## Stuck a pin in a careers book

KATHARINE HAMNETT CBE (b.1947)
*Cheltenham Ladies' College*

Champion of sustainable fashion, Hamnett says she plumped for a career in fashion after randomly sticking a pin into the fashion page in her school careers guide.

## A place in legal history

GINA MILLER (b.1965)
*Roedean School &*
*University of East London*

Miller secured a place in British legal history by successfully challenging the Conservative Government for triggering Article 50 without the approval of Parliament and for unlawfully proroguing Parliament in 2019. She was unable to finish her Law degree at the University of East London after she suffered a violent, racist attack. She returned to education later and gained a degree in Marketing and an MSc in Human Resource Management.

## An insult

AINSLEY HARRIOTT MBE (b.1957)
*Wandsworth Comprehensive &*
*Westminster Kingsway College*

When Harriott told his teacher he wanted to become a chef, the teacher replied, 'You're much too bright for that' which Harriott understandably describes as an insult to his profession.

## You're just a plain bun

PROF. DONALD MOSS (b.1935)
*Hackney Downs School &*
*Universities of Cambridge and London*

Professor Moss got a third-class degree at Cambridge. His careers office told him, 'When the ICIs and the Pilkington's come here, they take the chocolate eclairs and vanilla slices. You are just a plain bun.' Moss subsequently earned a PhD, a DSc and has published several respected books and papers.

**E. Hansell:** 'What does this "anti" attitude achieve? Who is impressed by it? Not the boys who are worth impressing. Not the other girls. If she doesn't change quickly there will be a lot of people with the thought "pity her poor husband".'

## Surviving not learning

DAVID OLUSOGA OBE (b.1970)
*Brighton Avenue Juniors & University of Liverpool*

Olusoga was educated 'despite school' and credits this to the tenacity of his mother and his history teacher Guy Falconer, who made history important to him. Olusoga tells of being taught by a teacher who drank from a British National Party mug and describes his school as racist and his days there as more about 'survival' than learning. Olusoga graduated in History and gained a postgraduate degree in Broadcast Journalism at Leeds Trinity.

# All you're good for is burgers

JACK MONROE (b.1988)
*Westcliff High School for Girls*

Monroe's head of year said, 'All you'll be good for is making burgers.' When her first cookbook *A Girl Called Jack* reached #1 in the UK charts, she sent the teacher a signed copy with the page for the burger recipe folded down and a note thanking her for the advice.

# Oxford only for the snob value

BRIDGET OSBORNE (b.1959)
*Redland High School for Girls & University of Oxford*

Former BBC producer Bridget Osborne is an example of why you should always follow your dreams. 'I got good O levels and my uncle suggested I apply to Oxford. I tentatively asked our careers mistress, who put a damper on the idea: "I don't know why on earth you want to do that? You're only doing it for the snob value and in any case you're not bright enough." Her comments just made me more determined to prove her wrong. Which I did. I got into Brasenose College, Oxford to study Politics, Philosophy and Economics (PPE).'

# A splendid person

THEO PAPHITIS (b.1959)
*Woodberry Down Comprehensive School*

Paphitis keeps his headmaster's final school report on his website: 'There is much in these reports for Theo to read carefully and dwell on. There are some very shrewd professional comments that cannot be ignored. A splendid person with fine qualities but unfortunately there are no examinations in this field.' Paphitis, who was dyslexic, says, 'A brilliant teacher can change your life forever, but one who writes you off prematurely can have one hell of an impact too ... Words can be a powerful tool for good or for bad in widening people's horizons or crushing their butterflies and we need to be mindful of that.'

# World's Most Influential Gap Year?

GRETA THUNBERG (b. 2003)
*Franksa Skolan & Kriglaskolen*

Thunberg disliked what she has called the 'monotony of school'. She sat at the back of her classes saying nothing. 'I thought I couldn't make a difference because I was too small.' In 2018, she organised a boycott at her school as a protest against climate change. She then took a 'gap year' from school to travel the world campaigning. She spoke at the UN Climate Action Summits, where she told the assembled politicians: 'You've stolen my dreams and my childhood. How dare you?'

**G. Higgins**: 'His only chance of getting into [University of] Bristol would be by breaking and entering.'

## Shot for wanting an education

MALALA YOUSAFZAI (b. 1997)
*Edgbaston High School for Girls &*
*University of Oxford*

Yousafzai, who won the Nobel Peace Prize in 2014, is better known simply by her first name: Malala. She is the young Pakistani woman whose support for female education made her the target of a Taliban assassination attempt in 2012. Aged just 15, she was shot in the head on a school bus. While recovering, she pleaded with the nurses to tell her father to bring her physics books because she was worried about falling behind. Malala went to Lady Margaret Hall, Oxford and graduated with a degree in Politics, Philosophy and Economics in 2020.

## WOMEN AND EDUCATION

**1714** Founding of Archbishop Tenison's Church of England High School, first co-ed school in the world.

**1868** The University of London becomes the first in the world to admit women.

**1870s** Women permitted to attend Cambridge lectures and sit exams but are NOT awarded degrees.

**1872** Girls' Public Day School formed to promote a modern education for girls.

**1897** A proposal to grant women at Cambridge formal recognition of their degrees led to a riot by angry male students.

**1898** Bedales becomes the first co-ed boarding school.

**1909** Ruckleigh becomes the first mixed sex preparatory school.

**1920** Oxford's women's colleges and halls gain 'full membership' of the University.

**1935** Kofoworola Moore (Lady Ademola) becomes the first black female to graduate from Oxford.

**1948** Cambridge begins awarding women degrees.

**2019** Number of female undergraduates entering Oxford matches male undergraduates.

# OLYMPIANS AND MUDDIED OAFS

*'The Battle of Waterloo was won on the playing fields of Eton.'*

ATTRIB: THE DUKE OF WELLINGTON

## Continually silly

DAVID BECKHAM OBE (b.1975)
*Chingford Foundation School*

Beckham always wanted to be a footballer. Like many young sportsmen and women, he faced careers officers understandably sceptical about the viability of a career in football or any other sport. Beckham, of course, succeeded mightily as a footballer and a model even though he did not pass a single O level. Years later, after trying to help his own children with their maths homework, Beckham remarked 'maths is totally done differently to what I was teached [*sic*] when I was at school.'

# Cheated at running

MALCOLM ALLISON (1927–2010)
*Central School, Bexleyheath*

Football player and manager Allison won the Victor Ludorum trophy at his junior school after deliberately tripping up his closest rival in a running race. He failed the entrance exam to the local grammar school because he wanted to play football instead of rugby.

# Powered by Prosecco

TONIA ANTONIAZZI MP (b.1971)
*St John Lloyd Comprehensive & University of Exeter*

Antoniazzi is a Welsh Rugby Union international and MP. She studied French, Italian and law at A level and read French and Italian at University of Exeter. Sport, however, was her first love: 'I did everything I could to avoid work at school. But I loved sport. At secondary school, the sports teacher – Mrs David – said I was the best netball player in the school. It was a statement of confidence in me which spurred me on. What I've learnt from this is: follow your passions. Give it a go. I'm still playing netball for a scratch team called Powered by Prosecco. As the name suggests, it's more about the social side of the game now, not so much winning at all costs!'

## Completely wasting his time

DUNCAN BELL (b.1974)
*Colston's School*

Rugby Union International Bell's school art report said, 'Duncan is lazy and silly. I find I don't trust him at all to get on, he lacks maturity and self-discipline. A disappointing year's work.' His religious education report said, 'His work leaves much to be desired. He is too content, in group work, to let the group do the work for him.'

## Swimming naked

TIM BENTINCK, 12TH EARL OF
PORTLAND MBE (b.1953)
*Harrow School & University of East Anglia*

In his autobiography *Being David Archer*, Bentinck says 'Sports were an important part of life at Harrow. I was quite good at most [but] I excelled at swimming. I learned how to swim fast from Pa, who had the most graceful freestyle stroke . . . [and had once] found himself in the thirties swimming naked against the Hitler Youth (swimming trunks were only made compulsory in the late 1950).' The school's pool was unheated at the time and Bentinck's father noted that 'extremely cold water has the same shrivelling effect on a Nazi as it does on a Harrovian'.

## Other schools wouldn't play with him

SIR DONALD BRADMAN (1908–2001)
*Bowral Public School*

Bradman is without doubt cricket's greatest batsman. Even at school he was prolific at scoring runs. Bradman put bowlers at rival schools to the sword so frequently that neighbouring schools refused to play Bowral if Bradman was in the team. Bradman left school at aged 14.

## Charlton Brothers

SIR BOBBY CHARLTON CBE (b.1937)
*Bedlington Grammar School*

Sir Bobby was once reprimanded by a teacher for staring out of the window during lessons. He was told he should focus on the blackboard because his future lay 'in your schoolwork' and not football. His brother Jack, who didn't go to grammar school, was punished for accidentally shooting a classmate with an air rifle. In later life, he became a passionate country sportsman and enjoyed game shooting.

## Not part of my schedule

MARCUS RASHFORD MBE (b.1997)
*Button Lane Primary & Ashton on Mersey*

England footballer and free school meal campaigner Rashford got nine GCSEs, though he has said that reading didn't play a large part in his 'schedule growing up'. He won an honorary degree from University of Manchester for forcing the Government into a U-turn on free school meals in 2020.

## The Flintoff gambit

ANDREW FLINTOFF MBE (b.1977)
*City of Preston High School*

'Freddie' Flintoff excelled at chess as well as academic and sporting pursuits. When playing chess for Lancashire against Staffordshire he noticed his opponent had not pressed his clock to mark the end of his move. Instead of flagging his opponent's mistake, Flintoff let the clock run down while he pretended to consider his own move. His opponent was timed out, burst into tears and Flintoff was rebuked by the Chess Federation for ungentlemanly conduct. One could argue that this was certainly not cricket.

---

**CRICKET AND THE ARTS**

Sir Aubrey Smith CBE captained England once before moving to Hollywood where he had a distinguished career acting English gentlemen. He went to school at Charterhouse and Cambridge. He founded the Hollywood Cricket Club, which still exists. Other theatrical types to play for the club were Sir Laurence Olivier, Boris Karloff and P.G. Wodehouse. Nobel Prize winning playwright Harold Pinter was another avid cricket fan; he captained and chaired The Gaieties, a wandering side. Samuel Beckett, playwright and Nobel Prize winner, is the only Nobel Prize winner to have played first-class cricket.

# It's not only cream that rises

RICHARD HELLER (b.1948)
*Repton School & University of Oxford*

Author and journalist Heller says, 'My earliest cricket master used to say: "Remember, you are the best player of your type in the world." Unfortunately, there has never been any demand for players of my type anywhere in the world.' Another teacher said to his maths set, 'Remember. It's not only the cream that rises to the top. It's the scum too.'

**T. Neville**'s son's cricket report said: 'He has enjoyed his time in the Colts game and, once he discovered his glasses, actually managed to stop or hit a moving ball. The mystery of throwing a ball still lies beyond some distant horizon.'

# A Maths maestro?

EMMA RADUCANU MBE (b.2002)
*Newstead Wood School*

Raducanu was a whizz for maths as well as tennis at school. She got an A* in mathematics and an A in economics in her A levels. She claims she was 'a numbers person' and maths was her favourite school subject. Virginia Wade, the last Brit to win the US Open before Raducanu, was also a mathematical maestro, graduating from the University of Sussex with a degree in Mathematics.

## A radio in his top hat

LORD SNOWDON, 1ST EARL OF
SNOWDON (1930–2017)
*Eton College & University of Cambridge*

Anthony Armstrong-Jones went to Eton, where he was skilled at gadgetry and carpentry, and built a radio set into the top hat which he wore about the school. His other boyish passion was rowing. He coxed Cambridge to victory in the 1950 Boat Race, while studying architecture at Jesus College. He is rumoured to have designed a special rudder for the boat, which was called the 'Banham Bombshell' and was very hard to steer. He never graduated from Cambridge, but maintained his passion for the Boat Race throughout his life.

# TOP TEACHERS AND TERRIBLE TYRANTS

*'I am indebted to my father for living, but to my teacher for living well.'*

ALEXANDER THE GREAT

## Wanted to be a footballer

DANNAHUE 'DANNY' CLARKE (b.1956)
*Various schools*

BBC TV's *Instant Gardener* got a Grade 1 in technical drawing at O level and remembers the encouragement of his design teacher in Germany – he came from an Army family and attended a number of schools around the world. 'I was good at drawing and enjoyed my technical drawing classes. My teacher encouraged me. It wasn't anything specific he said but you can tell when someone is rooting for you. I didn't know it at the time but now I realise that teacher and those technical drawing classes were the most important subject I studied at school.'

# Not doffing one's hat

GEORGE ABBOT (1562–1633)
*Royal Grammar School Guildford &*
*University of Oxford*

Abbot was a strict disciplinarian. So strict, in fact, that he had 140 boys at the University of Oxford imprisoned for failing to remove their hats while in his presence, which may be the highest number of students ever detained for the same offence at the same time. He is also the only Archbishop of Canterbury to kill another person while in office when he accidentally shot a man with his crossbow when hunting deer in 1621.


# I shut the door to keep my tutor out

DR ARASH ANGADJI (b.1979)
*Home schooled & Bradford College &*
*Queen Mary College, University of London*

Angadji was not an outstanding school student. 'I didn't like to study at all. My family hired a tutor to teach me at home. But I was so determined to avoid homework, I'd refuse to let him into the house. No tutor meant no lessons!' Arash was sent to Britain from Iran, aged 18. 'I needed to change my attitude. I realised qualifications were important if I wanted to make something of my life. I was on Jobseeker's allowance and was poor. So, I went to see Dr George Salmon at Bradford College. I told him my story and how much I wanted to study engineering and how hard I would work. To his eternal credit, he listened and enrolled me on the course. I eventually graduated with a merit. He believed in me and that has made all the difference to my life.'

## A shit teacher

GREG DAVIES (b.1968)
*Thomas Adams School & Brunel University*

Taskmaster Davies taught drama and English for 10 years before succeeding as a comic and actor. In one stand-up routine, Davies quotes a pupil he taught saying: 'Your lessons were a laugh, but let's be honest, you were a shit teacher.'

## Translates opera

RORY BREMNER (b.1961)
*Wellington College & King's College, London*

Satirist and impersonator Bremner graduated in French and German. At school, he was inspired to study languages by Derek Swift, a teacher whom Bremner described as 'superb'. Swift introduced Bremner to *Candide,* which was one of his inspirations to become a satirist. Because of his skill as a linguist, Bremner has been commissioned to translate operas such as *Carmen.*

**P. Hammond** recalls a favourite teacher reporting of a pupil who was regularly absent: 'I met him once and I was not impressed.'

## Stuck in second gear

ANDY STREET CBE (b.1963)
*Kings Edward's School Birmingham &
University of Oxford*

Now Mayor of the West Midlands, when Street was 15, a teacher wrote, '[he] is only in second gear.' Street agrees. 'I was a lazy schoolboy. I was not really motivated. But that changed in the sixth form when I met my economics teacher. He inspired me and suddenly I wanted to learn. So, it's true great teachers can change your life. My thanks go to Jack Cook – a brilliant provocateur and coach.' Street studied Politics, Philosophy & Economics at Keble College.

# Never give up

DEREK WYATT (b.1949)
*Colchester Royal Grammar School &*
*University of Oxford*

Wyatt, a former Labour MP, fluffed his A levels and exam to Oxford because he played too much sport. His headmaster consoled him: '"Never give up. You can do it and you will get there in the end."' This sentiment stayed with Wyatt. 'When things have been tough for me, I have always remembered his words. His timely intervention and his faith in me when I was down in the dumps made a massive difference, then and subsequently.' Wyatt persevered and went up to Oxford in 1981, winning a Blue in the Centenary Varsity Match, aged 32.

# SCIENTISTS, SCHOLARS AND TEACHERS' PETS

*'To spend too much time in studies is sloth; to use too much for ornamentation is affectation; to make judgement wholly by their rules is the humour of a scholar.'*

SIR FRANCIS BACON

## Lacklustre grades

ALEXANDER GRAHAM BELL (1847–1922)
*Royal High School Edinburgh &
Universities of Edinburgh and London*

Bell was taught at home before enrolling at the Royal High School where his record was undistinguished. In a history of the school, Bell is quoted as saying, 'My school life had been characterised by great indifference to the usual school studies and I took a very low rank in my classes. The subjects in which I really excelled, such as music, botany and natural history, formed no part of the main school curriculum.'

# Learnt to swear instead of studying

SIR JOHN BOYD ORR (1880–1971)
*Kilmarnock Academy & University of Glasgow*

Boyd Orr won the Nobel Peace Prize (1949) for his 'lifelong effort to conquer hunger and want'. From the start he was academically highly gifted winning scholarships and top honours at medical school. The only stain on his academic career happened when his father withdrew him from Kilmarnock Academy because he discovered Orr was learning swear words from the local quarry workers.

# Either you or the bear must go

FRANCIS BUCKLAND (1826–1880)
*Winchester College & University of Oxford*

Buckland was a practitioner of zoophagy (the eating of animals or animal matter), an interest he acquired from his father, a vicar who served battered mice, squirrel pie, horse's tongue and ostrich to his family. At Winchester College, Buckland developed his biological interest in animals, trapping mice, dissecting and some-times eating them. He went up to Christ Church in 1844. There, he kept a live bear in his college room, which almost got him expelled. His tutor wrote him an ultimatum, 'I hear you keep a bear [in your college rooms], Mr Buckland. Either you or the bear must go.'

## Lack of science

### CHARLES DARWIN (1809–1882)
*Shrewsbury School & University of Cambridge*

Darwin said of his boarding school, 'Nothing could have been worse for the development of my mind than Dr Butler's school, as it was strictly classical, nothing else being taught, except a little ancient geography and history. The school as a means of education to me was simply a blank.'

## A waste of time

### SIR JOHN GURDON (b.1933)
*Eton College & University of Oxford*

Gurdon's biology teacher said, 'I believe he has ideas about becoming a scientist; on his present showing this is quite ridiculous ... it would be a sheer waste of time, both on his part, and of those who have to teach him.' Gurdon went to Christ Church to study Classics but switched to

Zoology. Later, he framed the report and used it to remind him not to give up whenever he was facing challenges in his work and career. In 2012, he won the Nobel Prize for Medicine.

## You've got nine lives

KRISHNAN GURU-MURTHY (b.1970)
*Queen Elizabeth's Grammar School &
University of Oxford*

Channel 4 journalist Guru-Murthy took A level maths, chemistry, biology and general studies. When he failed his maths mock exam, he buckled down and passed the A level much to the surprise of his teacher who observed that Guru-Murthy was like a cat and 'always land on your feet.' Guru-Murthy went to Hertford College to study Politics, Philosophy and Economics.

## The Einstein of St Albans

STEPHEN HAWKING CBE (1942–2018)
*St Albans School & University of Oxford*

Unsurprisingly, Stephen Hawking was enormously clever from a young age and was nicknamed 'Einstein' at school. Hawking said of his school days that he loved pulling things apart but was not always so good at putting them back together again. He won a scholarship to University College, aged 17, and graduated with a first-class degree in Physics.

---

**FIRST SCHOOL NURSE**

Amy Hughes is regarded as the UK's 'first school nurse'. In 1892, she noticed children were absent from school because of minor ailments which could be addressed at school by a nurse, thereby, reducing 'sick days.' Her work no doubt influenced the Medical Inspection Act (1907) which forced local authorities to give children medical inspections at school.

---

## Unspoilt by his outstanding ability

SIR NICHOLAS HYTNER (b.1956)
*Manchester Grammar School &*
*University of Cambridge*

Hytner directed the original theatre production of *The History Boys*, Alan Bennett's play about the foibles of getting into Oxbridge. Like the boys in the play, Hytner went to Cambridge where he studied English at Trinity College.

His Universities and College Admissions Service (UCAS) report says: 'We were afraid, at one stage he might become somewhat spoilt by his quite outstanding ability as an actor but, in fact, he has turned into a very sound and conscientious Prefect and Sixth Former.' His school reports flag 'a genuine sense of style in writing, good logical capacity and [that he] is sensitively imaginative.'

**D. Duff**: 'His path is strewn with triumphs and records, and it is not for nothing that the question on everyone else's lips is "who's going to be second?".'

## A daftie

JAMES CLERK MAXWELL (1831–1879)
*Edinburgh Academy & University of Edinburgh*

When Einstein was asked if he 'stood on the shoulders of Newton' he replied that, in fact, he owed more to Maxwell's work in formulating the classical theory for electromagnetic radiation. At school, Maxwell was nicknamed 'daftie'. But at the age of 14 he wrote his first scientific paper, *On the Description of Oval Curves and those having a plurality of Foci*. Professor James Forbes, a scholar of the time, described the paper as 'very ingenious, certainly very remarkable for his years; and I believe, substantially new'.

## Neither a swot nor a dunce

SIR MICK JAGGER (b.1943)
*Dartford Grammar School &
London School of Economics*

Jagger got seven O levels and two A levels in English and history and is reputed to suggest this makes him neither a swot or a dunce. It was certainly good enough to get him into the London School of Economics (LSE) where he studied Finance and Accounting until he quit to pursue his music career.

## Best thing for TV is a science degree

MICHAEL OCKRENT (1946–1999)
*Highgate School & University of Edinburgh*

Mike Ockrent's work earned 13 Tony Awards nominations. He is well known for directing theatre and film hits such as *Educating Rita* and *Me and My Girl*. He is unusual among arts industry folk because he got three science A levels at school and studied Physics at the University of Edinburgh. After graduating, he applied to the ITV Directing School. He worried the artsy examiners would be put off by his scientific qualifications. 'I explained that ... putting on a play was rather like doing a scientific experiment. I likened the hypothesis to one's original concept of a play, the experiment was similar to the rehearsal, and I concluded by showing that "writing up one's results" was almost identical to the final performance.' He got the place.

## Merely recollected

WILLIAM PITT THE YOUNGER (1759–1806)
*Home schooled & University of Cambridge*

William Pitt the Elder vowed he would never send his son to Eton, his alma mater, because he had 'hardly known a boy whose spirit had not been broken at Eton' and that 'a public school might suit a boy of turbulent disposition but would not do where there was any gentleness.' Instead, Pitt the Younger was home schooled. His tutor, the Reverend Edward Wilson, said of him, he 'never so much learned as merely recollected'. Pitt went to Pembroke College, aged 13. He then became the youngest British Prime Minister at the age of 24 in 1783.

# Running through the wheat fields

THERESA MAY MP (b.1956)
*Wheatley Park School & University of Oxford*

May is probably the least naughty British Prime Minister of all time, as perhaps a vicar's daughter should be. During the 2017 General Election, she was asked to reveal the worst thing she had ever done at school. Her reply that she and her best friend used to run occasionally through the nearby wheat fields to the anger of the local farmers provoked widespread mockery. Her goody two shoes answer may even have contributed to her losing her majority at the next election.

# 'God has arrived'

LUDWIG WITTGENSTEIN (1889–1951)
*Home schooled & Various universities*

Wittgenstein said of his *Tractatus Logico-Philosophicus* that it solved the known problems of philosophy 'on all essential points'. At the end of his interview at Cambridge, at which he discussed his thesis with Bertrand Russell and G. E. Moore, both considerable philosophers themselves, Wittgenstein got up and patted their shoulders saying, 'Don't worry, I know you'll never understand it.' His arrogance was often remarked upon, including by economist John Maynard Keynes who noted in his diary on meeting Wittgenstein: 'Well, God has arrived. I met him on the 5.15 train.'

## A pleasure to share in his thinking

SIR JOHN REDWOOD MP (b.1951)
*Kent College, Canterbury & University of Oxford*

Redwood's final school report says, 'Once and for all I must say what a pleasure it has been to know him and to share a little in his studies and his thinking. I admire his high standards of both scholarship and behaviour. I hope that experience will show him new excellencies and perfections and deepen that great kindness within which he already has at heart.' Redwood is a distinguished fellow of All Souls College, Oxford.

**C. Topping**: 'How typical of Topping, when discussing the latest fuel cells being used by NASA in the space program, to announce loudly to the class that "Chemistry has not changed in 100 years!"'

# THE GREAT BRITISH PUBLIC

*Honestly, who hasn't had a bad school report? The reports in this section come from ordinary folk around the country who were prepared to share their shame for the amusement of the nation. Some were even willing to put their names to them.*

**Anon**: 'A tendency to the slang phrase as well as the pretentious.'

**G. Anderson**'s woodwork: 'Too poor for restrained comment.'

**W. Buller**'s French: 'His total inability to retain the simplest facts for any length of time precludes any progress.'

**Anon**: 'Affects too great a detachment.'

**M. Burton**: 'When others are inventing a suitable answer using their common sense, he tends to stare round with an expression of ill-used despair on his face.'

**D. Calder**, of a pupil whose French accent was 'appallingly Kiwi': 'It would be better if [he] spoke English in Paris lest he upset the French.'

**D. Chandler**: 'You have covered most of the essential points, but you express yourself very badly and more than once talk nonsense.'

**Anon**: 'His position in the class is due to his irregularity, unpunctuality, and want of attention. If he ever knew what he had to do, had books with which to do it, and could think of it while doing it, he might rise in the division for he has quite as much sense as those around him.'

**M. Clifford**: 'His mind burns with the tiny gleam of a glow worm, scarcely noticeably. I hope it will shine with a stronger, clearer and brighter light as he gets older.' On the plus side, 'His ears are busier than his mouth: a refreshing quality.'

**N. Embricos**: 'He's a courteous and genial fellow to deal with. But . . . by persisting to draw attention to himself with his current hair-cut and dirty clothing and affected diction he is likely to become a "marked man" in the college.'

**Anon**: 'He has tended to adopt a silly approach to his achievements even to the extent of making a mock show of delight in low marks.'

**I. Garner**: After coming second from bottom, his Latin teacher wrote, 'He was beaten of his rightful place by one.'

**D. Goldberg**'s brother: 'A cheerful optimist like Goldberg should have something to be optimistic about!'

**Anon**: 'I was delighted to hear of his reborn enthusiasm for cricket and am only sorry that Jupiter Pluvius has so frequently frustrated his ambitions this summer.'

**N. Gowing**: 'At the Picton dance, where he was meant to be a waiter, he showed total lack of inhibition and I literally had to prise him apart from one of the visiting girls and remind him that his place was in the kitchen!'

**Anon**: 'The pointless flamboyance must cease.'

**M. Harrison**: 'I am counting on the fact he has the moral fibre to realise that a fundamental change of approach is required.'

**Anon**: 'His written work is liable to contain wild and inconsistent errors.'

**A.C. Hartley**: 'His project work was an oasis in a desert of mediocrity.'

**T. Hickson** recalls a colleague writing: 'He can do this subject standing on his head, and often does.'

**C. McCooey** wrote of a pupil: 'Her appetite for chocolate pudding is not matched by hers for this subject.'

**P. MacGowan**: 'Answers questions parrot-fashion; unfortunately, it's a parrot with a bad memory.'

**D. Peart** reports a fellow pupil was described as: 'A dull boy who brightens at the sight of food.'

**Anon**: 'It is impossible to suppress a certain anxiety. He is clearly far from ready to face the A levels and the hope he will produce some miraculous burst of energy over the remaining weeks seems remote.'

**K. Reffell** reports fellow pupil received the feedback: 'There is too much ego in his cosmos.'

**A. Rowell**: 'It's quite simple, when Rowell wants to speak, I shut up; sadly when I want to speak, he doesn't, and therefore takes up his usual repost in the corridor.'

**Anon**: 'Once or twice when his mind could be caught, he answered questions sensibly in my examination, but it is certainly a process to attract his attention at present. His viva-voce was generally very wild.'

**A. Smith**: 'Empty vessels make the most sound.'

**Anon**: 'There has been a cheerful absence of effort in all his work.'

**P. Walter** of an unnamed pupil: 'The dawn of legibility reveals a total inability to spell.'

**C. Wells**: 'Unlike the poor, your son is seldom with us.'

**Anon**: 'Has shown in all his work a good-humoured consciousness that he was going to leave at the end of the term.'

**M. Winwood**'s headmaster wrote of a school dandy only: 'Luke 12:27'. The Bible verse cited reads, 'Consider the lilies of the field, how they grow: They toil not, nor do they spin. But I say to you, not even Solomon in all his glory was arrayed as one of these.'

**Anon**: 'His first essay was interesting but rather wild. Subsequent work has been pedestrian. I preferred the first essay, whatever its faults.'

# REFERENCES

Arch. George Abbot: Donaldson, W., *Brewer's Rogues, Villains & Eccentrics.* Cassell, 2002.

Prince Albert Victor: Royal Archives, Windsor.

Eric Ambler: Colfe School Archive & Ambler, E., *Here Lies Eric Ambler.* Penguin, 1986.

Herbert Asquith: Alderson, J. P., *Mr. Asquith.* Methuen, 1905. Qtd. Oxford Dictionary of National Biography [online], 2022.

Stanley Baldwin: Harrow Association records.

David Beckham: Russell, G., *Arise Sir David Beckham: Footballer, Celebrity, Legend – The Biography of Britain's Best Loved Sporting Icon.* John Blake, 2011.

Alexander Graham Bell: Murray, J., *A History of the Royal High School.* Edinburgh, Royal High School, 1997.

Tim Bentinck: *Being David Archer: and other unusual ways of earning a living.* Constable, 2017.

Humphry Berkeley: *The Life & Death of Rochester Sneath.* Harriman House, 2009.

Sir Richard Branson: *Losing my Virginity.* Virgin Books, 2009.

Charlotte Brontë: Romantics and Victorians Collection, British Library.

David Bowie: The Headmasters Blog. 2019.

Baroness Rosie Boycott: Sale, J., 'Passed / Failed: University was a very druggy place.' *The Independent*, 15.04.2004.

Francis Buckland: Bompas, G., *Life of Frank Buckland*. Smith, Elder, & Co. 1888.

Lewis Carroll: Dodgson Collingwood, S., *The Life and Letters of Lewis Carroll*. 1898. Accessed online through Project Gutenberg.

Sir Winston Churchill: *The Harrovian*, 1929.

Samuel Taylor Coleridge: *Biographia Literaria*. Accessed online through Project Gutenberg.

Benedict Cumberbatch: O'Toole. L., 'There was pressure on me to get brilliant A levels.' *Metro*, May 2013.

Charles Darwin: *Autobiographies of Charles Darwin*. Penguin Classics, 2002.

Sir Alec Douglas-Home: Connolly. C., *Enemies of Promise*. George Routledge & Sons, 1938.

Greg Davies: 'On being the world's worst teacher' via *YouTube*.

Laurence Fox: *The Harrovian*, 1995.

Giles Fraser: Open University Digital Archive, September 2015.

Krishnan Guru-Murthy: Sale, J., 'Passed/Failed: An education in the life of …' *The Independent*, 18.03.2010.

Arthur Harding: *My Apprenticeship to Crime*. Bishops Gate Institute, 1998.

Ainsley Harriott: Hind, J., 'My sister takes control of my cooking at home'. *Observer*, 21.03.2021.

Gerard Manley Hopkins: Letter dated 1862, qtd. Highgate School Magazine Archive.

Sir Nicholas Hytner: Manchester Grammar School Archive.

John Lennon: Scheff., D. *All We Are Saying: The Last Major Interview With John Lennon and Yoko Ono*. St Martin's Press, 2000.

Joanna Lumley: *Absolutely: A Memoir*. Weidenfeld & Nicholson, 2011.

Miriam Margolyes: 'Naughty Miriam: Why Oxford High
    School never left Miriam Margolyes'. *Girls School Day
    Trust* [online], 22.05.2019.

Sir Jonathan Miller: St Pauls' School Archive.

Michael Ockrent: *The Cholmeleian.*

Thomas Paine: Thetford Grammar Archive.

Sir Harold Pinter: Clove Club Archives; Supple, B., *Doors
    Open.* Asher, 2009; Billington, M., *Harold Pinter.*
    Faber & Faber, 2007.

Queen Elizabeth I: Ascham, R., *The Scholemaster.* 1570.
    Accessed online through Project Gutenberg.

Sir Terence Rattigan: *The Harrovian.*

Baroness Margaret Thatcher: Young, H., *One of Us.* Pan
    Macmillan, 1990.

Edward Thomas: St Pauls Archive.

Sandi Toksvig: '"I played hooky for years" – Sandi
    Toksvig on What She Learnt at School.' *Teachwire,*
    1.09.2018.

Anthony Trollope: *An Autobiography.* Google Books, 1883.

# BIBLIOGRAPHY

BBC Scotland. *Billy and Us*, 2020.

Downer, M. *The Sultan of Zanzibar: The Bizarre World
    & Spectacular Hoaxes of Horace de Vere Cole.* Black
    Spring, 2010.

Hattersley, R. *David Lloyd George: the Great Outsider.*
    Abacus, 2010.

Higham, C. *Mrs Simpson: Secret Lives of the Duchess of
    Windsor.* Pan Macmillan, 2016.

Ridley, J. *The Heir Apparent: A Life of Edward VII, the Playboy Prince*. Random House, 2013.

Scott, W, ed. *The Works of Jonathan Swift*. Ulan Press, 2012.

Thomas-Symonds, N. *NYE: The Political Life of Aneurin Bevan*. I.B.Tauris, 2016.

Thunberg, G. *No One Is Too Small to Make a Difference*. Penguin, 2019.

Turner, D. *The Old Boys: The Decline and Rise of the Public School*. Yale University Press, 2015.

Vegas, J. *Becoming Johnny Vegas*. Harper Collins, 2014.

Whipplesnaith. *The Night Climbers of Cambridge*. Oleander Press, 2007.

**James Thellusson** has written for *The Oldie* and other magazines. He went to St Paul's School, London and then York University. In both places, he could have tried much harder. After a career in journalism and PR, he now blogs as his alterego Man in the Middle, a bemused Boomer struggling to balance the demands of family life and his own desire to spend his remaining years selfishly and recklessly. The spark for this book was lit when he found his old school reports in the attic during the first Covid lock down.

*www.sandstonepress.com*

Subscribe to our weekly newsletter for events information,
author news, paperback and e-book deals, and the occasional
photo of authors' pets!
**bit.ly/SandstonePress**

 facebook.com/SandstonePress/

 @SandstonePress